COUNTRIES IN OUR WORLD

EGYPT

Ali Brownlie Bojang

W
FRANKLIN WATTS
LONDON•SYDNEY

First published in 2010 by
Franklin Watts
338 Euston Road
London NW1 3BH

Franklin Watts Australia
Level 17/207 Kent Street
Sydney NSW 2000

Produced for Franklin Watts by
White-Thomson Publishing Ltd
+44 (0) 845 362 8240
www.wtpub.co.uk

Series consultant: Rob Bowden
Editor: Sonya Newland
Designer: Clare Nicholas
Picture researcher: Amy Sparks

A CIP catalogue record for this book is available
from the British Library.

Dewey Classification: 962'.05

ISBN 978 0 7496 9200 1

Printed in Malaysia

Franklin Watts is a division of Hachette Children's
Books, an Hachette UK company

www.hachette.co.uk

Contents

Egypt boasts one of the oldest civilizations in the world, dating back more than 5,000 years. Modern Egypt is an exciting mix of traditional and modern cultures, of rich and poor, and of city and countryside. It is a major player in the politics and trade of both Africa and the Middle East.

IT STARTED HERE

Early civilization

Egyptian civilization contributed the first organized government to the world. Ancient Egyptians also developed methods of irrigation to help grow their crops, and they used the earliest known alphabet.

Where in the world?

Egypt is one of only three countries in the world (the others are Turkey and Russia) that lie on two continents. It is situated in north-east Africa and on the Sinai Peninsula, which is part of Asia. Although clearly an African country, the Middle Eastern influence is strong in Egypt. As well as its land borders, Egypt is bordered by the Mediterranean Sea in the north and by the Red Sea in the east.

An ancient civilization

One of the world's earliest civilizations grew up on the banks of the River Nile in Egypt. The river gave the ancient Egyptians water to grow their crops, and the surrounding desert provided protection against attack from other peoples. For 3,000 years, Egyptian culture – based on a religious belief in the afterlife – flourished.

▼ *Egypt has land borders with the Gaza Strip and Israel to the north-east, Sudan to the south and Libya to the west.*

The Egyptians built huge pyramids, sphinxes and statues as tombs and monuments to their rulers, called pharaohs.

Influences and occupations

From 341 BCE, Egypt was ruled by a series of invaders from Persia (now Iran), Greece and Rome. In the seventh century, the Arabs came to Egypt and introduced the Islamic religion and the Arabic language. The Arabs ruled Egypt for the next 600 years, until the Turks conquered them in 1517 and took control of Egypt.

IT'S A FACT!

The Great Pyramid of Giza is the only one of the Seven Wonders of the Ancient World that is still standing. It is 147 m (482 ft) tall, and was the tallest monument in the world until the nineteenth century.

▼ *In the desert outside Cairo stand remains of the ancient Egyptian civilization – the Sphinx and the Great Pyramid of Giza.*

Britain and Egypt

During the nineteenth century, both France and Britain took an interest in Egypt, and helped to pay for the building of the Suez Canal in 1869. This created a 163-km (100-mile) 'short-cut' from Europe to India and the rest of Asia. Ships no longer had to go all the way around Africa. This was very important to countries like Britain that were trying to increase their influence over world trade. In 1882, Britain seized control of the Egyptian government to safeguard its interest in the Suez Canal. For the next 70 years Britain had some control over Egypt, although there was still an Egyptian king and an Egyptian prime minister and parliament.

GOING GLOBAL

The Suez Canal is an important trade route. In 2008, an average of 1,780 ships a month passed through it. Between 2000 and 2008, the amount of shipping from Southeast Asia and the Far East, including China, passing through the canal increased by two-and-a-half times. This shows how important the Suez Canal has been for Chinese exports to Europe.

▼ *A container ship passes through the Suez Canal. Fourteen per cent of total world trade and 26 per cent of world oil exports travel via this waterway.*

The Egyptian republic

In 1952, a group of soldiers led by Gamal Abdel Nasser staged a revolution. They intended to overthrow the king, Farouk, who they thought was corrupt and too influenced by the British. The revolution was a success and the monarchy was abolished. In 1953, the new Egyptian republic was born.

▲ *Gamal Abdel Nasser (waving), leader of the revolution and second president of Egypt, drives through the streets of Cairo.*

Egypt's place in the world

Egypt is still a major channel for international trade. The country's role as a go-between and mediator in the Middle East is also becoming more important, as problems between its neighbours Israel and Palestine worsen. Egypt has a good relationship with the USA – which it supported during the Gulf War in 1990 – and the European Union (EU), as well as being a key player in the Arab world.

BASIC DATA

Official name: Arab Republic of Egypt	
Capital: Cairo	
Size: 1,001,450 sq km (386,662 sq miles)	
Population: 83,082,869	
Currency: Egyptian pound	

Landscapes and environment

Egypt is a plateau made up of sand and rock. Across this dry landscape flows the longest river in the world, the Nile, and on either side of the river are fertile valleys. The Nile is the lifeline of Egypt, providing water for drinking and crops.

The River Nile

The Nile flows for 1,545 km (960 miles) through Egypt, creating a green line through the desert. In the past the river would flood every year and leave behind a fine fertile silt. This created an area up to 12 km (7.5 miles) either side of the river where farming could take place. With the help of irrigation, people were able to grow a wide variety of crops, such as cotton, rice, corn, wheat, beans, fruit and vegetables. They also kept cattle, water buffalo, sheep and goats. Today, the flooding of the Nile is controlled by the Aswan High Dam.

IT'S A FACT!

The Nile Delta, where the river spreads out and flows into the Mediterranean Sea, is one of the largest deltas in the world. It covers 240 km (150 miles) of the Mediterranean coastline and is about 160 km (100 miles) from north to south. The Nile Delta is the winter home of some of the largest groups of birds in the world, including little gulls and whiskered terns.

▼ *Traditional Egyptian boats, called* feluccas, *sailing on the Nile.*

Climate

There is very little rainfall in Egypt and everywhere is hot and dry. The capital, Cairo, receives no more than around 10 mm (0.4 in) of rain a year, which usually falls in the cool season between December and February. Further south the amount of rainfall decreases even more, and in some desert locations it may rain only once every few years. During April, dust storms are common, caused by the hot Sirocco wind that blows from the Sahara Desert.

▲ *Tourists protect their faces from the sand and dust in Cairo.*

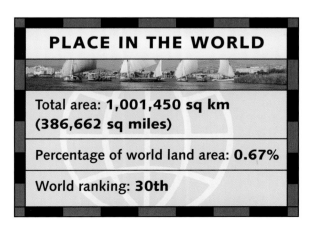

PLACE IN THE WORLD

Total area: **1,001,450 sq km (386,662 sq miles)**

Percentage of world land area: **0.67%**

World ranking: **30th**

The deserts

About 95 per cent of Egypt is desert. In this harsh environment, where temperatures can reach over 50°C (122°F), very few plants, animals or people can survive. To the west lies the Western Desert, which is actually part of the Sahara Desert – the largest desert in the world. This is a relatively flat area, covering about two-thirds of the country, where strong

▲ *In Egypt's deserts, the wind creates limestone rock formations and high sand dunes.*

winds have blown the sand into dunes more than 30 m (100 ft) high – as tall as a 10-storey building. Here, the wind also forms large limestone outcrops. To the east of the country lie the more rocky and mountainous Eastern and Sinai deserts.

Highs and lows

The highest point in Egypt is Mount Catherine, which lies towards the southern tip of the Sinai Peninsula and is 2,629 m (8,625 ft) high. Mountainous peaks running down the coast of the Red Sea reach 750 m (2,461 ft). In the Western Desert there are vast low-lying hollows. The largest of these is the Qattara Depression, a huge area of saltpans and rocks. At 133 m (436 ft) below sea level, this is the second-lowest point in Africa.

Environmental problems

Egypt's exceptionally dry climate and its large population create huge demands for water and fertile land. Vital farmland is being taken over by the growing cities and, in some places, lost to the deserts. To produce more food from less land, farmers use more fertilizers and pesticides on their crops. These pollute the River Nile, adding to the pollution from sewage and waste from the cities. The Red Sea, with its coral reefs, is also threatened by oil pollution and increasing tourism.

IT'S A FACT!

Global warming is causing sea levels to rise, threatening Egypt's low-lying but densely populated delta area and the ability to grow crops there, as well as destroying many of its ancient structures. Scientists predict that by 2020, more than 15 per cent of the valuable delta area will have been lost, and use this as a warning to other countries about what may happen if climate-change issues are not addressed.

▼ *This area of the Nile Delta could be flooded in a few decades as a result of global warming.*

Population and migration

Egypt's population of around 83 million is the largest of any Arab-speaking country, and the second largest in Africa after Nigeria. Most of the people live on the small strip of land around the River Nile. Egypt's population is growing very rapidly.

Who are the Egyptians?

Egypt's inhabitants are a mix of races, descended from the ancient Egyptians, Berbers from other parts of North Africa and sub-Saharan Africans such as the Nubians. There are also groups descended from the Arabs, Greeks and Turks. Most Egyptians live along the fertile banks of the River Nile and in its delta. There are small communities of people in the oases of the Western Desert and in the oil-drilling and mining towns of the Arabian Desert.

PLACE IN THE WORLD

Population: **83,082,869**	
Percentage of world total: **1.14%**	
World ranking: **16th**	

▼ *Nubia covers part of southern Egypt and stretches into northern Sudan. Here, a Nubian woman collects water from a canal running through her village near Aswan.*

12

City living

Over 40 per cent of the population lives in cities such as Cairo, Alexandria, Subra al-Haymah and Luxor. Egypt's cities have grown quickly. In 1850 the population of Cairo was 250,000; today it is around 17 million and it is the largest city in Africa. The populations of the cities swell daily as people commute to work from the towns and villages nearby.

Population density

About 95 per cent of Egyptians live along the Nile, on about three per cent of the land area. This concentration has created one of the most densely populated areas in the world. On average there are 1,540 people per sq km, while the density in the whole of Egypt is 77 people per sq km. In comparison, the population density of the UK is 246 and for Africa as a whole it is 65 people per sq km.

IT'S A FACT!

In the deserts of Egypt live small groups of Bedouins. Although they are divided into different tribes, they have several similar customs and are known for their folk music and dance. In the past, Bedouins were nomadic – they moved around throughout the year – but today many of them live in permanent settlements in desert areas, and some have also now settled in Egypt's large cities.

▼ *Alexandria is the second largest city in Egypt, with a population of more than 4 million.*

Population growth

Egypt's population has grown very rapidly in recent years. It more than doubled between 1970 and 2000. Although the rate at which it is growing has slowed down now, it is still increasing by about 1.5 million people every year. One-third of Egyptians are under 14 years old, and in the near future they will be looking for work, houses and healthcare, as well as schools for their own children.

Pastures new

Job opportunities in Egypt are scarce and salaries are low. Many Egyptians leave the country to find work and higher wages in Saudi Arabia and other countries in the Middle East, Libya, the USA or Europe. In 2009, it was estimated that 3 million Egyptians were working in other countries. Some of these people are well-qualified, working in jobs such as engineering and teaching.

▼ *Although life expectancy at birth is quite high (72.2 years), Egypt has an extremely young population. Only 4.8 per cent of the population are over 65.*

Desperate to leave

Others have little education and few skills, and in their desperation to improve their lives they cross the Mediterranean Sea to Europe on makeshift boats. It is a dangerous journey, and some die on the way when their boats sink. Some travel to Egypt from other countries especially to take this boat journey, if they are unable to leave from their own countries. Illegal immigration like this has risen over the past 10 years, but it is impossible to know how many people have successfully reached and settled in Europe. Some experts think it may be as many as 20,000 people a year.

GOING GLOBAL

The money that Egyptians living abroad send home is very important to their families and to Egypt as a whole. In 2007, Egyptians sent home nearly US$6 billion, which has helped the Egyptian economy.

▼ *Illegal immigrants from Egypt and other countries in North Africa arrive in Italy.*

Culture and lifestyles

Egyptian culture is a mix of the old and the new. It has absorbed ideas and traditions from its invaders and visitors over thousands of years, and combined these with its own ancient traditions.

Religion

The Arabs introduced Islam to Egypt in the seventh century, and today times of business meetings, films and concerts are decided by the sound of the call to prayer from the minarets five times a day. Ninety per cent of Egyptians are Muslim. In recent years some Egyptians have started to support a stricter form of Islam, and more and more women are covering their heads and faces with a veil, or *hijab*. Most other people – around nine per cent – are Coptic (Egyptian) Christians, making up the largest Christian population in the Middle East.

▶ *A mosque in the city of Hurghada on the Red Sea coast. This mosque is quite modern – built around 30 years ago – but Islam has been the main religion here since the seventh century.*

IT STARTED HERE

Writing

It is thought that the first true alphabetic writing started in Egypt in around 2000 BCE, based on an even older system of hieroglyphs – small pictures used to represent words. Experts think that most alphabets in the world today are based on the ancient Egyptian system of writing.

Family and food

Family is important to all Egyptians, although today Egyptian families are getting smaller, as people are choosing to have fewer children. Food is an important part of the hospitality shown to visitors in Egypt. Typical dishes are made from beans and lentils, rice and flatbreads, and vegetables cooked in onions and tomatoes. Egyptian food is similar to that in neighbouring countries such as Greece, Lebanon and Turkey. In the cities, however, wealthy Egyptians frequently eat European food. French cuisine and Western fast food are particularly popular.

IT'S A FACT!

All Egyptian children must attend school between the ages of six and 14. Education is free in government-run schools, although there are private schools available for the children of wealthier Egyptians. Arabic is the official language in Egypt, but many schools also teach French and English.

▼ *Western-style fast food is popular in Egypt's large cities. This sign for McDonald's is written in Arabic, Egypt's official language.*

GOING GLOBAL

Many ancient Egyptian objects, such as statues of pharaohs and mummies, can be found in museums all over the world. Some of the best examples are in the British Museum in London, the New York Metropolitan Museum of Art and the Louvre in Paris. Touring exhibitions, such as those showing the treasures of the pharaoh Tutankhamen, have been sell-outs in countries such as the UK and USA.

▲ *This obelisk, known as Cleopatra's Needle, once guarded an ancient temple at Luxor. Now it stands in Paris's Place de la Concorde.*

Life in the countryside

Country life in Egypt is very different from life in the cities. In the Nile Delta, for example, there are still peasant farmers, called *fellahins*, wearing the traditional baggy trousers. Most people in rural areas are very poor.

Life in the cities

In contrast, life in the cities is similar to that in cities all over Europe and the USA. Busy urban areas such as Cairo and Alexandria are packed with people. There are traffic jams, blaring horns, office buildings, shopping malls and restaurants. Despite these signs of Western life, however, only a few of Egypt's city dwellers are as wealthy as Europeans or Americans, and standards of living in Egyptian cities are lower than in these countries.

Music

Traditional music in Egypt has been influenced by Arabic music from Persia and India, and its tones and rhythms are very different from Western music. This music is usually played at weddings and other festivals, but young Egyptians prefer pop music, and there are many modern pop singers in Egypt today. Many of these base their music on the traditional forms. Two of the most popular singers are Mohamed Mounir and Amr Diab.

THE HOME OF...

Arabic films

Egypt has been nicknamed the 'Hollywood of the Arab world', and is the major supplier of films in this region, producing around 40 a year. An international film festival is held every year in Cairo, and this has gained renown not just among Arab countries, but also those in the Western world.

Sport

Football is the most popular sport in Egypt, both for playing and watching. Egyptian football clubs, especially El Ahly and El Zamalek, are known throughout the Middle East and Africa. The national team is popularly known as The Pharaohs, and it is the most successful African football team, having won the African Nations Cup six times. Other popular sports in Egypt are basketball, handball, squash and tennis. Egyptian runners are also admired all over the world for their speed and stamina.

▼ *Egypt's national football team celebrates winning the African Nations Cup in 2008 after the final against Cameroon.*

Only three per cent of Egypt's land can be used to grow crops, but 32 per cent of the population is involved in farming. The activities that bring in the most foreign money to Egypt are the production and export of oil, tourism, money sent home from Egyptians working abroad and fees from shipping companies using the Suez Canal.

Natural resources

Oil is Egypt's most valuable natural resource, and in the 1990s Egypt also began exporting natural gas. Both of these are mined near the Red Sea, on the Sinai Peninsula and in the Western Desert. Phosphate rock (used to make fertilizer), iron ore and salt are also mined in Egypt. Egypt is self-sufficient in energy, which means it does not rely on other countries for its energy needs. As well as oil, Egypt generates hydroelectricity using the enormous Aswan High Dam. The dam is used to control the Nile floods. However, it also stops some of the silt from being carried down the river, which means the soil in some areas is not as fertile as it used to be.

▼ *The Aswan High Dam provides around 20 per cent of Egypt's electricity, but it has caused concern because of the effect it has had on the quality of soil downriver.*

Farming

Nearly all farms in Egypt are located in the Nile Valley and Delta. Traditional farms are small and are irrigated with water from the Nile. On larger, more commercial farms, the land is worked more intensively and fertilizers are used to get the most crops possible. There are usually two crops a year and the main cash crop – crops grown especially for export rather than for personal use – is cotton. Some desert land is being developed for farming, but these schemes are very expensive. Water has to be either transported by pipes from the Nile, or very deep holes have to be dug to reach underground water supplies.

GLOBAL LEADER

Egyptian cotton

Egyptian cotton is considered to be the best in the world. It is used to produce high-quality sheets for top department stores, and clothes for many well-known high-street shops. However, it is estimated that about a million children in Egypt are employed to help with the cotton harvest, often working in very bad conditions.

Trade

Egypt buys more from other countries than it sells to them, which is one reason why Egypt is in debt. Egypt exports its oil and ready-made clothes, cotton and other farming products such as citrus fruit and rice. It sells these mainly to the USA and Italy. It buys food, machinery and transport equipment mainly from China, France, Germany, Italy and the USA.

▶ *Workers in a t-shirt factory. Clothes are big business in Egypt because of the high-quality cotton that can be grown there.*

Industry

Egypt has some manufacturing industries in cities such as Cairo and Alexandria. These produce mainly iron and steel, textiles, plastics and cars. There are also several oil refineries. Some international companies, such as car manufacturers, have been attracted to Egypt because it has such a large population, which not only provides buyers for the manufactured goods, but also workers who can be paid low wages compared to what the companies would pay for labour in their own countries.

Small businesses

Small businesses can be found in many of Egypt's city streets. Here, people may repair household items or cars, recycle metal, litter or fabrics, or sell all different products either in small shops or on market stalls. Many of these businesses are not registered and people do not pay their taxes. It is impossible to know how many people work in this informal way, but the number has been estimated at 7 million.

GLOBAL LEADER

Mubarak Pumping Station

The Mubarak Pumping Station is the largest in the world. It pumps water from Lake Nasser to the Toshka Depression, a large low-lying area of desert. The pump facility is 30 m (100 ft) wide, 140 m (460 ft) long and 60 m (197 ft) high. It was built in a pit around 15 storeys deep, and is 10 times the size of a football stadium.

▼ *In the markets of Egypt, vendors sell locally made handicrafts such as textiles and objects crafted from metal.*

▲ *The clear, warm water and the variety of fish and coral reefs of the Red Sea offer some of the best scuba diving in the world.*

Tourism

With its good weather, fascinating history, monuments such as the pyramids and the temples, and its beautiful Red Sea resorts such as Sharm-el-Sheikh and Dahab, Egypt is one of the world's top tourist destinations. Tourism is a vital source of foreign income for the country's economy. In 2007, more than 10 million tourists visited Egypt and contributed 11 per cent to Egypt's total income, or gross domestic product (GDP).

THE HOME OF...

Scuba diving

The year-round high temperatures, low rainfall, warm seas and beautiful coral reefs have enabled the Red Sea town of Sharm el-Sheikh to develop from a small fishing village into one of the world's top scuba-diving resorts.

The largest numbers of tourists come from Italy, followed by visitors from Germany, the UK and France. The Egyptian government is concerned that fewer tourists may visit Egypt in the coming years because of the bad state of the global economy.

Egypt is a republic, which means it is not ruled by a monarch, but by representatives elected by the people. It has a president and prime minister who share power. Since independence in 1953, Egypt has had close connections with different world powers.

Ruling Egypt

The responsibility of ruling Egypt is shared between the president and the prime minister. However, the president holds a lot of power because he supervises how the country's laws are drawn up. He is also in charge of Egypt's armed forces, which puts him in a very strong position.

▼ *Egyptian soldiers set off to support US troops during the First Gulf War in 1990.*

The first president

In 1953, when Egypt became independent, the leader of the revolution, Gamal Abdel Nasser, became its president. He was very powerful and tried to stop the influence that many foreign countries had over Egypt, especially the UK. He wanted to unite all the Arab nations under Egyptian control, so he turned to the USSR for help. This did not please countries in the West, because they were not on good terms with the USSR.

Al-Sadat and Mubarak

The next president, Anwar al-Sadat, distanced Egypt from the USSR and tried to make peace with Israel. This angered some Egyptians and he was assassinated in 1981. The current president, Hosni Mubarak, has worked hard to build Egypt's strength in the Arab world and has developed good relations with the West.

FAMOUS EGYPTIAN

Anwar al-Sadat (1918–81)

In 1978, President Anwar al-Sadat received the Nobel Peace Prize for his role in improving relations between Egypt and Israel, which he shared with the Israeli prime minister, Menachem Begin. However, in 1981 he was killed by assassins from secret groups who wanted to make Egypt a pure Islamic society and who felt he had betrayed Egypt and Islam.

▼ *Anwar al-Sadat (left), shortly before he was assassinated. Hosni Mubarak is on the right.*

Egypt and Israel

For many years Egypt and Israel were sworn enemies, and between 1948 and 1978, the two countries fought three wars. However, in 1978, US president Jimmy Carter brought together the warring sides. As a result, a peace treaty was signed between Egypt and Israel, making Egypt the first Arabic-speaking country to recognize Israel as a nation in its own right. Since then Egypt has played an important role as a mediator, or go-between, between Israel and the Palestinian people.

Human rights

Several international human rights organizations, such as Amnesty International and Human Rights Watch, have criticized Egypt's record on human rights. People who disagree with the president have been put in jail and tortured. Women do not have the same rights as men, particularly when it comes to marriage and divorce. More and more women in Egypt are calling for equal rights with men, and are starting to take a more active part in politics.

▼ *Egyptian journalist Yomna Mokhtar used the social networking site Facebook to campaign for rights for unmarried women, who are regarded as inferior in Egypt.*

International links

Egypt is a member of several influential international organizations, including the Arab League, the African Union and the United Nations. Membership of these groups allows Egypt to have a say about many international issues, and to play a significant role in world events, such as trade agreements and peacekeeping missions in troubled countries.

▼ *Boutros Boutros-Ghali (left) on a visit to Rwanda during his time as Secretary-General of the United Nations.*

FAMOUS EGYPTIAN

Boutros Boutros-Ghali (b. 1922)

Boutros Boutros-Ghali was born in Cairo in 1922. He was an Egyptian diplomat and became the sixth Secretary-General of the United Nations, holding this position from January 1992 to January 1997. During his time as Secretary-General he had to deal with issues such as the Rwandan genocide, the Angolan Civil War and the wars in the former Yugoslavia.

Egypt in 2020

One of the biggest challenges Egypt faces is the need for land and water to provide for its growing population. This issue could be made more difficult by the threat of climate change.

The need for land

As the overcrowded cities of Egypt continue to expand, they will take up valuable farming land. To solve this problem, the government has started some major projects to develop the deserts. By 2017, it estimates that it will have converted 1.5 million hectares (3.5 million acres) of dry, sandy desert into productive farmland. Water for these projects is provided by deep wells that tap into a huge water reserve beneath the Sahara Desert.

▲ *As Egypt's population continues to grow, slums are springing up on the outskirts of the cities. Providing adequate housing is a priority for the Egyptian government.*

The need for water

As Egypt's population grows there will be a greater need for water for homes, for crops, for factories and to create power. One big concern is what countries up-river on the Nile do to affect the waters. As they take more

water to fulfil their own needs, for example, it may decrease the amount of water available to the Egyptians. Although there is an agreement in place about water use, some experts think tension over water could lead to the world's first 'water war'.

Climate change

Climate change, and the rise in sea levels, is a major threat to the food-producing Nile Delta region. Scientists have predicted that the Mediterranean will rise between 30 cm (12 in) and 1 m (3 ft) by the end of the twenty-first century. This would flood coastal areas along the Delta.

Developing a modern country

For thousands of years Egypt has faced the limitations of its deserts and climate. By and beyond 2020 it will continue to face these – and other – challenges. However, its already strong influence, particularly in the Middle East, is likely to develop further in the near future, helping Egypt become an even more important player on the world stage, too.

▼ *Dealing with the dry climate is one of Egypt's biggest challenges, but ancient treasures such as the pyramids and great temples will continue to attract tourists and boost the economy.*

Glossary

Arab someone who belongs to a race of people that originated in the Arabian Peninsula.

cash crops crops that are grown especially to be exported to other countries.

Christianity a religion that follows the teachings of Jesus Christ.

coral reefs underwater structures formed from the remains of sea creatures.

economy the financial system of a country or region, including how much money is made from the production and sale of goods and services.

export to transport products or materials abroad for sale or trade.

feluccas traditional Egyptian sailing boats with flat bottoms and triangular sails.

global warming the gradual rise in temperatures on the surface of the Earth, caused by changes in the amount of greenhouse gases in the atmosphere.

gross domestic product (GDP) the total amount of money a country earns every year.

immigrant a person who has moved to another country to live.

irrigation supplying dry land with water by means of ditches and channels.

Islam a religion with belief in one god (Allah) and his last prophet, Muhammad.

Muslim a follower of the Islamic religion.

nomadic moving from place to place, often to find the best grazing land for herds of livestock.

oasis a fertile or green area in a desert where there is a source of water.

plateau a raised area of land, usually fairly flat and sometimes also called 'tableland'.

pollution spoiling the environment with man-made waste such as vehicle emissions, waste gases from factories, or chemicals from fertilizers.

population density the number of people living in a square kilometre or square mile of a country.

pyramids large structures built as tombs for the ancient Egyptian pharaohs.

republic a form of government in which a country is ruled not by a king or queen, but by officials elected by the people.

rural relating to the countryside.

saltpans small, undrained, shallow depressions where water builds up and evaporates, leaving salt behind.

silt fine particles of earth deposited by rivers.

Further information

Books

*The Changing face
of Egypt*
by Ron Ragsdale
(Wayland, 2007)

*Egypt (Letters from Around
the World)*
by David Cumming
(Cherrytree Books, 2005)

Welcome to Egypt
by Nicole Frank and
Susan L. Wilson
(Franklin Watts, 2006)

Egypt (Cultures of the World)
by Patricia Levy and S. Levy
(Marshall Cavendish, 2007)

Settlements of the River Nile
by Rob Bowden
(Heinemann, 2006)

We're from Egypt
by Victoria Parker
(Heinemann Library, 2005)

Websites

http://www.touregypt.net/Kids/
A site for children offering a virtual tour of Egypt, with information about its history and monuments as well as games and activities.

http://www.horus.ics.org.eg/en/Default_HTML.aspx
The Little Horus website, where readers are guided through information on Egypt by the sky god.

**http://www.travelforkids.com/Funtodo/Egypt/
egypt.htm**
Take a journey through Egypt with this fun site, from Cairo to the Valley of the Kings.

**http://www.socialstudiesforkids.com/subjects/
economics.htm**
Get to grips with economics on this site where topics such as money, trade and budgets are explained.

Every effort has been made by the publisher to ensure that these websites contain no inappropriate or offensive material. However, because of the nature of the Internet, it is impossible to guarantee that the content of these sites will not be altered. We strongly advise that Internet access is supervised by a responsible adult.

Index

Numbers in **bold** indicate pictures

Water and Fibre
for a Healthy Body

Angela Royston

Heinemann LIBRARY

www.heinemann.co.uk/library

Visit our website to find out more information about **Heinemann Library** books.

To order:

☎ Phone 44 (0) 1865 888066

 Send a fax to 44 (0) 1865 314091

 Visit the Heinemann Bookshop at www.heinemann.co.uk/library to browse our catalogue and order online.

Heinemann Library is an imprint of Capstone Global Library Limited, a company incorporated in England and Wales having its registered office at 7 Pilgrim Street, London, EC4V 6LB – Registered company number: 6695582

"Heinemann" is a registered trademark of Pearson Education Limited, under licence to Capstone Global Library Limited

Text © Capstone Global Library Limited 2003, 2009
Second edition first published in hardback in 2009
Second edition first published in paperback in 2009
The moral rights of the proprietor have been asserted.

Edited by Louise Galpine, Catherine Clarke, and Claire Throp
Designed by Victoria Bevan and AMR Design Ltd
Original illustrations © Capstone Global Library Ltd
Illustrated by Geoff Ward and BigTop p.37
Picture research by Mica Brancic
Originated by Steve Walker
Printed and bound in China by CTPS

ISBN 978 0 431 16726 8 (hardback)
13 12 11 10 09
10 9 8 7 6 5 4 3 2 1

ISBN 978 0 431 16732 9 (paperback)
13 12 11 10 09
10 9 8 7 6 5 4 3 2 1

British Library Cataloguing in Publication Data
Royston, Angela
Water and fibre. – 2nd edition – (Body needs)
613.2'87
A full catalogue record for this book is available from the British Library.

Acknowledgements
We would like to thank the following for permission to reproduce photographs: ©Corbis: pp. **8**, **15**, **22**, **27**, **28** (Sygma/Jean Pierre), **30**, **33**; ©Gareth Boden: pp. **5**, **6**, **12**, **34**, **40**, **41**; ©Liz Eddison: pp. **9**, **14**, **39**, **42**; ©Photodisc: pp. **38**; ©Photolibrary Group Ltd: pp. **7** (Imagestate RM/Foodfolio Foodfolio), **10** (Fancy/Tomas Rodriguez), **29** (Radius Images), **32** (Fresh Food Images/Roger Stowell); ©SPL: pp. **18** (Eye of Science), **19** (Biophoto Associates), **31**, **35** (CNRI); ©Trevor Clifford: p. **24**.

Cover photograph of red apple being peeled, reproduced with permission of ©PhotoLibrary Group/Foodpix/Burke/Triolo Productions.

We would like to thank Dr Sarah Schenker for her invaluable assistance in the preparation of this book.

Every effort has been made to contact copyright holders of any material reproduced in this book. Any omissions will be rectified in subsequent printings if notice is given to the publishers.

Disclaimer
All the Internet addresses (URLs) given in this book were valid at the time of going to press. However, due to the dynamic nature of the Internet, some addresses may have changed, or sites may have ceased to exist since publication. While the author and publishers regret any inconvenience this may cause readers, no responsibility for any such changes can be accepted by either the author or the publishers.

Contents

Any words appearing in the text in bold, **like this**, are explained
in the glossary.

Why do we need to eat?

You need to eat and drink to stay alive. All of the food you eat contains **nutrients**, which your body uses to get **energy**, to grow new **cells**, and to get the chemicals it needs to work properly. If your body lacks nutrients, you will become ill.

Nutrients

Nutrients are divided into groups, according to what they supply. **Carbohydrates** and **fats** supply energy. **Proteins** supply **amino acids**, which are the building blocks needed to make new cells and repair old cells. **Vitamins** and **minerals** supply chemicals that the cells need to function properly. Most foods contain a mixture of nutrients, but many are particularly rich in one kind.

Energy foods

Your body uses energy all the time. Running, walking, and activities that involve moving around use up more energy than quieter activities, such as thinking, eating, and breathing, but even sleeping uses up some energy. Most of your energy comes from the carbohydrates and fats that you eat. Carbohydrates include potatoes, rice, and food made from wheat, such as bread and pasta. Sugar is also a carbohydrate, so biscuits, cakes, and sweets all give you energy. However, energy from sugary foods does not last long.

Fats

Fats come from animals and from plants. Butter, milk, and cheese contain quite a lot of animal fat, while margarines and oils are made from plants. The body stores any extra fat you eat as a layer of fat under the skin and within the body.

YOU ARE WHAT YOU EAT

Your body is composed of the same kind of nutrients that you eat. Muscles are mainly protein, while your bones contain the minerals calcium and phosphorus. Under your skin is a layer of fat that helps to keep you warm.

Proteins

Much of your body is made of protein, so, as old cells wear out and die, the body needs constant supplies of new protein to build new cells. While you are still growing, your body needs extra protein to create millions of extra cells. Meat, fish, milk, and beans are all good sources of protein.

This family is enjoying a meal that is rich in nutrients. Although we say they are enjoying spaghetti with bolognese sauce, they are really taking in carbohydrate with protein and vitamin sauce.

Vitamins and minerals

Most foods contain small amounts of vitamins and minerals. Minerals include **zinc**, **calcium**, **iron**, and **phosphorus**. Fruit and vegetables contain several vitamins and minerals. Milk and cheese contain different ones. Your body only needs small amounts of these chemicals, so, provided you eat a wide range of food in adequate amounts, you will get all the vitamins and minerals you need.

Water and fibre

We usually think of healthy food as food that contains plenty of nutrients, but this book looks at two essential ingredients that are not nutrients: water and fibre. They are not nutrients because they do not supply energy, or help the growth of new cells, and they do not contain vitamins and minerals that the cells need to function. However, water in particular is essential for us to live, and fibre is necessary to help keep your bowels healthy.

Water

Up to 60 per cent of your body is water. Body fluids like blood, **urine**, digestive juices, and **mucus** are all mainly water. But all cells contain water, so even the parts of the body that look solid, such as muscles, skin, and other **organs**, contain water, too.

Losing water

Your body is losing water all the time, mainly through urine and sweat. You need to take in clean water to replace the water that is lost every day. If you do not drink enough, you can become **dehydrated**. A person can survive for several weeks without food, but your body quickly becomes dehydrated and you would die after a few days without water.

Body fact

If you weigh 42 kilograms (93 pounds), about 28 kilograms (62 pounds) of that is made up of water. This means that your body contains about 28 litres (49 pints) of water.

Drinking plain water is the best way to take in water, but most drinks and many foods contain water, too.

Fibre

Fibre is the parts of plants that your body cannot **digest**. It consists mainly of the hard walls of plant cells. At one time people thought that fibre was simply waste that the body could do without, but then scientists realized that fibre is needed to keep the digestive system healthy and working well. Fibre helps the body to get rid of **faeces** more quickly.

The digestive system

The digestive system breaks up food into pieces that are small enough so that the nutrients in the food can pass into the blood. Most digestion takes place in the **small intestine**. Any food components that are not digested pass through the **large intestine** and collect at the end. They are expelled from your body through the anus when you go to the toilet.

Getting rid of waste

Both water and fibre are important in getting rid of waste. Faeces are easier to expel if they are moist and soft. Fibre absorbs water and so makes the faeces bulkier and softer.

Eating an orange is a good way of taking in fibre and liquid. The drops of orange juice are held together by a thin film or membrane. The membrane is fibre that is not digested.

What is water?

Water is made up of just two **elements** — **hydrogen** and **oxygen** — combined together. Both of these elements are normally gases, but when they combine together they form a liquid. Many substances **dissolve** easily in water and so water usually contains other chemicals, too. Some of these chemicals are minerals that your body can use. In contaminated water there are **bacteria** and **pollutants** that cause harm.

Calcium in water

Some water contains a lot of calcium. Calcium is a mineral that makes your bones and teeth strong. The disadvantage is that it makes the water "hard", and leaves a hard, chalky-white deposit in kettles and in pipes. It takes more soap to get a lather in hard water.

Bacteria in water

Bacteria, like many forms of life, need water to live and breed. Typhoid, cholera, and dysentery are three serious illnesses that are carried by water. They are caused by bacteria and kill thousands of people every year. The water you drink must be treated to kill bacteria, and this treatment makes it safe to drink.

Tap water

The water that comes out of your taps has been treated before it is piped to homes and other buildings. The **sediments** are filtered out of the water. A chemical called chlorine is added to kill any bacteria. In some places the mineral fluoride is added, too. Fluoride can help protect your teeth from tooth decay and it is also added to most toothpastes.

 Water is treated to make it safe to drink before it is piped to your home.

Water filters

Some people do not like the taste of tap water. Water filters reduce the amount of calcium and chlorine in the water. Some people think that this makes the water "softer" and that it tastes nicer, too.

Bottled water

Some companies produce bottled water that has been collected from underground springs. Many people think that bottled water tastes better than tap water. However, bottled water is expensive and many people consider it an unnecessary luxury.

 This jug contains a water filter. It is used to filter tap water.

Water fact

The water you drink is the same water that the dinosaurs drank! Earth's water is constantly **recycled**. It **evaporates** from the oceans and falls as rain. Some of the rain runs into reservoirs, wells, and underground springs. The rest flows into rivers and back to the oceans.

Water in food

Even solid foods contain a lot of water. This is because all food comes from plants, **fungi**, or animals. Like all living things, they consist mainly of water. Some foods contain more water than others. Leafy vegetables, such as lettuce and watercress, have the most — they are over 90 per cent water.

Plants

Plants take in water from the soil through their roots. Dissolved in the water are nutrients that the plant needs to remain healthy. The water and nutrients travel through narrow tubes up the stem to the leaves. Here, some of the water combines with **carbon dioxide** from the air to make food, using the energy of sunlight. The sugary food is carried to all other parts of the plant — the flowers, fruit, stem, leaves, and roots.

Fruit juice

Fruit contains seeds that can grow into new plants. Some plants surround the seeds with sweet, juicy flesh. This kind of fruit contains a lot of water and is often made into fruit juice. The fruit of apples, oranges, pineapples, peaches, mangos, and blackcurrants, for example, are squashed and the juice is collected and sold in bottles or cartons.

VEGETABLE OR FRUIT?

Although we think of cucumbers, aubergines, peppers, and tomatoes as vegetables, they are really fruits. You can see the seeds inside them.

You can squeeze oranges to make orange juice. When the squeezing has finished, the only solids left will be the skin, the pith, and the seeds.

Other food from plants

Nuts, grains, peas, and beans are seeds, too. They contain water, but not as much as juicy fruits. Most vegetables come from other parts of the plant and they are all rich in water. Cabbage, watercress, and lettuce are leaves and contain the most water. Broccoli and cauliflowers are flowers, while celery and asparagus are stems. Some plants store food in their roots. Potatoes and onions are two examples of root vegetables. Some vegetables, such as carrots and beetroot, are juiced and sold as drinks.

Food from animals

Meat and fish are more than half water, but meat contains much less water than fruit and vegetables. Female cows, sheep, and goats make milk that we drink or make into cheese and yoghurt. Milk is about 90 per cent water, so when you have a drink of milk you are drinking mainly water. The other 10 per cent consists of fat, sugar, and protein, as well as vitamins and minerals.

Dried food

Sometimes food is dried to preserve it. Raisins and sultanas are different kinds of dried grapes. Even so, these foods still contain some water. Dried dates, for example, are 15 per cent water.

This chart shows the percentage of water in various kinds of foods.

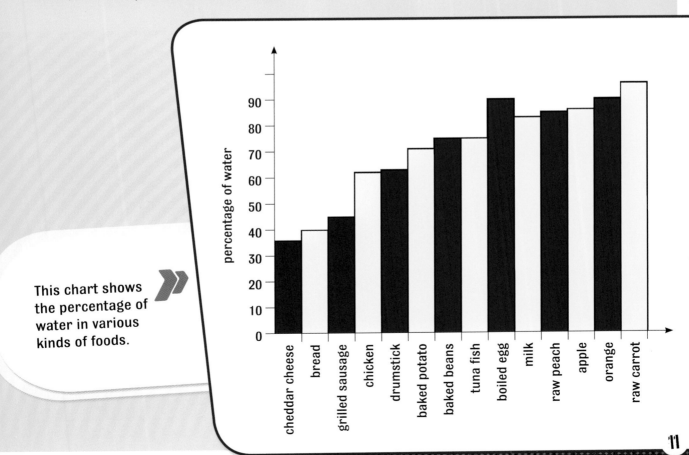

What is fibre?

Fibre is the term given to a mixture of substances, mainly complex carbohydrates. These cannot be digested in the small intestine in humans, but pass into the large intestine where they are broken down. Fibre can be classified as **insoluble**, such as **cellulose**, or **soluble**, such as pectin, depending on whether or not it dissolves in ethanol (a type of alcohol).

Insoluble fibre

Cellulose is a strong, rubbery material that forms the walls of all the cells that make up a plant. Leaves, stems, flowers, fruits, and roots all contain cellulose. Plant cells are too small to see and so you cannot see all the fibre in a plant, but some plants contain hard or stringy parts that are easy to see. Celery and rhubarb, for example, are stems and they have stringy bits that run from one end to the other. Seeds, particularly beans and grains, are often protected with a tough outer skin that is rich in cellulose. The skin of an apple, for example, or a potato, contains more fibre than the rest of it.

Digesting cellulose

Cellulose is a carbohydrate that cows, sheep, and other grazing animals can digest. Humans, however, cannot digest cellulose because the human digestive system does not contain the **enzymes** that are needed to break it down. This means that although fibre is mainly carbohydrate, eating it does not give you any energy.

When you cut up runner beans, you can easily see the stringy fibres that give the beans their strength. But the tough skin that covers broad beans (also shown here) contains cellulose, too.

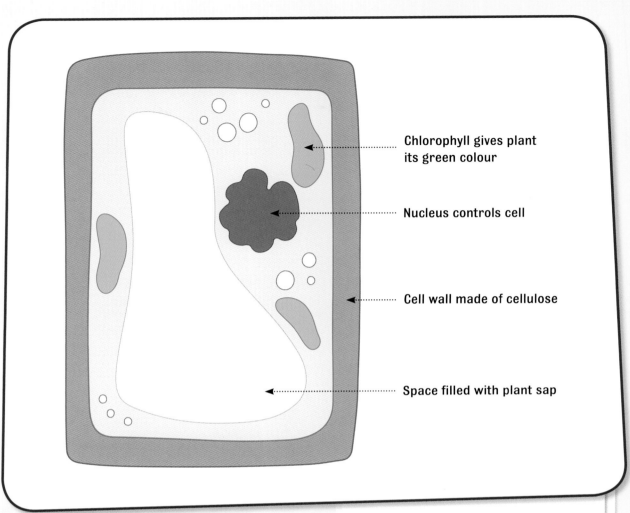

Chlorophyll gives plant its green colour

Nucleus controls cell

Cell wall made of cellulose

Space filled with plant sap

 The walls of plant cells are made of cellulose. Some parts of the plant have thick cell walls containing extra cellulose.

Chewing

Cellulose is very tough, so it is difficult to chew. It takes longer, for example, to chew up a mouthful of raw carrot than it does to chew a piece of chocolate. After chewing, you also have more to swallow. Chewing helps your digestive system because it breaks up the food into smaller pieces before you swallow it, making it easier to digest. In addition, the more you chew, the more **saliva** your mouth makes, and saliva contains an enzyme that starts to digest other carbohydrates.

Soluble fibre

Soluble fibre includes pectins and gums found in fruits, such as apples, and vegetables, such as turnips and sweet potatoes. It is also present in oats. Soluble fibre in the diet can help to reduce the amount of **cholesterol** in the blood.

Fibre in food

Although you can clearly see stringy bits in many vegetables, the foods that are richest in fibre are nuts, dried fruit, beans, lentils, and peas. Foods made from grains, such as rice and wheat, which are made into bread and pasta, are also full of fibre. Rice and wheat, however, are often processed so that most of the fibre is taken out of them. This is called refining.

Nuts and dried fruit

Nuts are the seeds of some trees. They include coconuts, hazel nuts, walnuts, almonds, and pine nuts. Nuts are rich in fibre, protein, and oils, which are a kind of fat. Dried fruits include dates, prunes, and desiccated (dried out) coconut. Raisins, sultanas, and currants are all different types of dried grapes.

Pulses

Pulses are seeds from pods, such as beans, lentils, and peas, and are rich in protein as well as in fibre. Other pulses are made into tasty dishes. The Indian food dahl is made from lentils mixed with spices and the dip houmous is made mainly from chickpeas.

 These foods are all rich in fibre.

In many countries, grains are ground by hand. This means that all of the grain is used and the flour is full of nutrients and fibre.

Grains

Grains come from cereal crops, such as wheat, rice, oats, maize, and barley. Breakfast cereals, as the name suggests, are made from cereal grains. The grains we eat most are wheat and rice. Wheat is ground into flour that is used to make bread, pasta, cakes, and biscuits. Rice is normally eaten as a grain with meat or vegetables. How much fibre we get from grains depends on how much of the grain is used in the food. Brown rice and wholegrain foods use all of the grain and so contain more fibre than white rice and refined flour.

Wholegrain and refined foods

Wholemeal flour is ground from whole grains of wheat and is made into wholemeal bread, wholemeal pasta, and other wholemeal products. Most white flour, pasta, and white bread is made from wheat from which much of the fibre has been removed. All bread and pasta, however, contains some fibre.

Food with no fibre

Many foods contain almost no fibre at all. Milk and other dairy products, meat, and fish contain no natural fibre. Many other foods, such as chocolate, fizzy drinks, some biscuits, and cakes, have had all or nearly all the fibre taken out.

BROWN BREAD OR WHOLEMEAL?

Most wholemeal breads are brown, but not all brown breads are wholemeal. You have to look on the wrapping to see how much fibre a loaf of bread contains.

What happens in the digestive system?

The job of the digestive system is to break up the nutrients in food into pieces that are small enough to pass through the walls of the gut and into the bloodstream. Carbohydrates, fats, and proteins are broken down into separate **molecules**, and even, in the case of protein, into parts of molecules. Water molecules are so small they pass easily into the blood, but with fibre the opposite is true. It cannot be broken down small enough and so is not absorbed and passes right through the digestive system.

In the mouth

Digestion begins in the mouth. The teeth slice, chop, and grind the food into smaller pieces that mix with saliva to make a soft mush. Chewing is particularly important in breaking up fibre. It makes the fibre soft and easy to swallow. When the mouthful of food has been chewed enough, your tongue pushes it to the back of your mouth and you automatically swallow it.

In the stomach

The mushy pulp passes down your throat, through the **pharynx**, and into the **oesophagus**, the tube that joins your mouth to your stomach. The walls of the stomach make a strong acid, called hydrochloric acid. This acid usually kills off any germs in the food and starts to break the proteins up into separate molecules. Your stomach is a stretchy bag that stores and churns the food for a few hours. The mushy pulp gradually changes into a kind of thick soup, called **chyme**. Every so often, some of the chyme squirts from your stomach into the small intestine.

Body fact

In adults, the length of the digestive tube from the mouth to the anus is about 9.5 metres (31 feet) long. In children it is shorter. Multiply your height by 5.5 to get a rough idea of the length of your digestive tube.

In the small intestine

The small intestine is a long thin tube. As chyme passes into the tube, it mixes with digestive juices that come from the **liver**, the **pancreas**, and the walls of the small intestine. The juice from the pancreas **neutralizes** the acid of the stomach juice. This lets the enzymes in all the digestive juices get to work on the food, breaking up the carbohydrates, proteins, and fats. Gradually these nutrients pass through the walls of the small intestine into the blood. The remainder, mainly fibre, digestive juices, and water, passes from the small intestine into a wider tube called the large intestine.

The digestive system breaks up food using mechanical and chemical processes. It changes the food from a bite-sized chunk of, for example, peanut butter sandwich into a mushy pulp, and then into a soupy liquid.

The digestive system

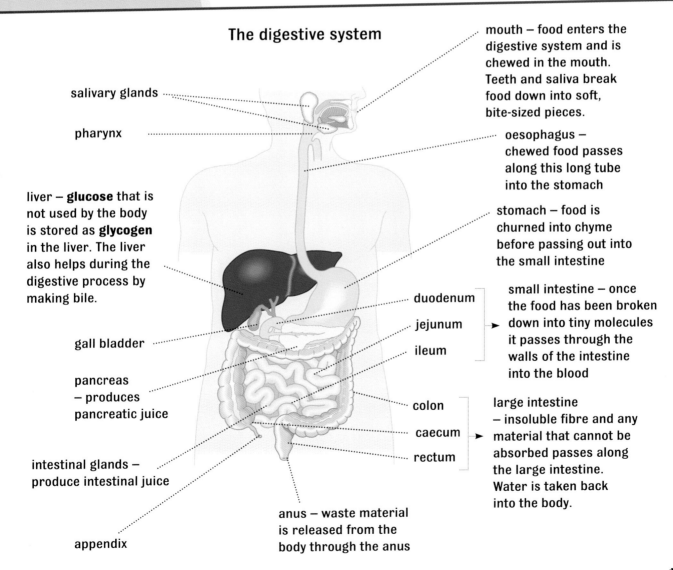

salivary glands

pharynx

liver – **glucose** that is not used by the body is stored as **glycogen** in the liver. The liver also helps during the digestive process by making bile.

gall bladder

pancreas – produces pancreatic juice

intestinal glands – produce intestinal juice

appendix

mouth – food enters the digestive system and is chewed in the mouth. Teeth and saliva break food down into soft, bite-sized pieces.

oesophagus – chewed food passes along this long tube into the stomach

stomach – food is churned into chyme before passing out into the small intestine

duodenum

jejunum

ileum

small intestine – once the food has been broken down into tiny molecules it passes through the walls of the intestine into the blood

colon

caecum

rectum

large intestine – insoluble fibre and any material that cannot be absorbed passes along the large intestine. Water is taken back into the body.

anus – waste material is released from the body through the anus

Digesting water and fibre

Water passes easily through the walls of the digestive system into the blood. Some of it is absorbed in the stomach, but more is absorbed in the small intestine. The rest combines with fibre to form a mushy paste that passes into the large intestine. Here more water is absorbed through the walls of the tube and the paste gradually becomes more solid.

Fibre in the small intestine

Carbohydrates are broken up in the mouth, in the stomach, and in the small intestine. Fibre, however, is not able to be digested and absorbed in the small intestine and passes largely unchanged into the large intestine.

Fibre in the large intestine

The undigested fibre travels slowly through the large intestine and forms one of the main components of faeces. Faeces, however, is not simply fibre and water. It also contains digestive juices, mucus, dead cells from the walls of the digestive system, and bacteria from the large intestine.

The wall of the small intestine is lined with tiny bumps called villi. The villi provide a bigger surface area for absorbing nutrients.

Hostile environment

The digestive system is a hostile and harsh environment. The enzymes and acid in the juices, which break down food so efficiently, can also attack the living cells of the digestive system itself. The walls of the stomach and intestines are protected by mucus. The lining of the stomach and intestine have a rapid turnover of cells, which means the cells only last a few days. As the cells die, they join the undigested waste.

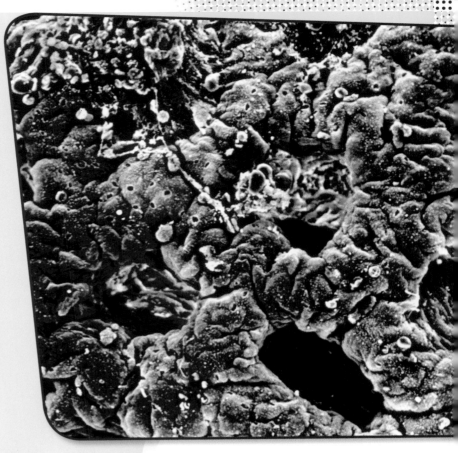

Water

As water is absorbed through the lining of the stomach and intestine, it can carry with it water soluble vitamins and minerals. More water is absorbed in the large intestine. Provided the body is not short of water, enough remains in the large intestine to make the faeces soft and moist.

 This high magnification scan shows the mucus lining of the large intestine. Mucus helps the faeces move and protects the wall of the intestine from damage.

Getting rid of faeces

Of all the food you eat, only a small fraction completes the whole journey through the digestive system. Faeces are stored at the end of the large intestine. It moves from there into the rectum and is then expelled from the body through the anus. A tight muscle in the anus relaxes to allow the faeces to pass through.

TIME IN TRANSIT

Most undigested food takes about ten hours to reach the large intestine. It may take up to another 20 hours before it finally leaves the body.

Using fibre

Most fibre is insoluble fibre. It is not digested and passes through the intestines with all the other waste matter. Fibre makes the waste matter, called faeces, bulkier. Bulky faeces helps the large intestine (also called the bowel) to work better and helps to keep it healthy. Some fibre is soluble.

A long and winding journey

The small intestine is coiled within the folds of the large intestine. Food has to make its way through all the coils into the large intestine. Undigested food and waste then have to travel upwards – against **gravity** – along and down to reach the anus, the final exit. The process by which food and waste are moved through the digestive tubes is called peristalsis.

Peristalsis

The walls of the gut contain circular bands of muscles. When a band of muscle contracts it pushes the food forwards. At the same time, the band of muscle in front of the food relaxes, allowing the food to slide through it. The movement of each muscle relaxing and then contracting passes along the tube like a wave. The muscles in the small intestines work continually, churning the food around the tube, but the muscles in the large intestine work much more slowly.

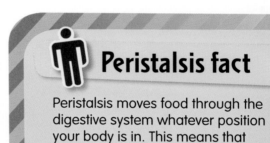

Peristalsis fact

Peristalsis moves food through the digestive system whatever position your body is in. This means that even if you are upside-down you can still digest food.

Healthy bowels

If you eat plenty of fibre and drink plenty of water you are likely to empty your bowels about once a day. This keeps the muscles of the large intestine healthy, and helps keep a healthy balance of bacteria in the bowel. Some people go to the toilet more often and some people go less often than once a day. What matters most is that the waste material is bulky and easy to push out of the body.

Absorbing cholesterol

Oats and certain fruits and vegetables contain soluble fibre. Soluble fibre can bind to bile acids that are released into the small intestine to help digest fat. These bile acids cannot then be reabsorbed. Instead they pass into the large intestine where they form part of the faeces. This means that more stored cholesterol in the blood has to be used to make new bile acids. This is how soluble fibre in the diet helps to lower blood cholesterol levels.

Food moves through all the tubes in the digestive system in much the same way as you squeeze toothpaste out of a tube. Valves separate one stage of the digestive system from the next. They allow food to travel only in one direction – unless you are vomiting!

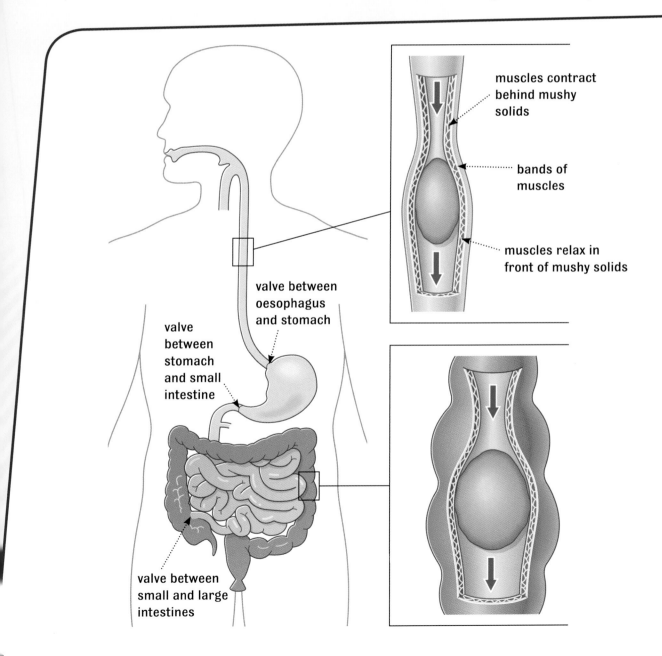

muscles contract behind mushy solids

bands of muscles

muscles relax in front of mushy solids

valve between oesophagus and stomach

valve between stomach and small intestine

valve between small and large intestines

Water in the body

Water is the main ingredient of all the different fluids in the body, including digestive juices, blood, sweat, and urine. Each of these liquids needs water to make them runny. In addition, all the organs and tissues inside your body are coated with moisture. Salty water inside and outside the cells allows nutrients and chemicals to enter and leave each cell. Water is also involved in many of the chemical reactions that take place inside the body.

Digestive juices

Digestive juices, produced in the liver and pancreas, trickle through narrow tubes and into the small intestine. They join other digestive juices made in the mouth, stomach, and in the walls of the intestines.

Hitching a ride

Minerals, such as salt, and some vitamins can only be taken into the body along with water. They dissolve in water and pass with it into the blood.

Blood

The clear, watery part of blood is called plasma. This clear liquid has sugar and other nutrients dissolved in it. Red blood cells take in oxygen in the lungs. As the blood circulates around the body, every living cell is provided with a constant supply of food and oxygen.

Drinking plenty of water helps to keep your skin moist and healthy. It also helps all the cells in your body work better.

Water in the cells

Water plays an important role in helping nutrients and oxygen pass from the blood into each cell. Chemical reactions inside the cells change glucose and oxygen into energy, while other reactions allow the cell to carry out its own particular tasks. Many of these chemical reactions involve water. Water then helps carbon dioxide and waste chemicals pass from the cell into the blood to be taken away and expelled from the body.

Water fact

Your body makes 10 litres (17.6 pints) of digestive juices every day. Most of this is water that is reabsorbed into the body.

Urine and sweat

Waste chemicals are carried away from the cells by the blood and leave the body in urine or sweat. Urine is made in the kidneys (see pages 26 and 27), while sweat is made in the sweat glands and is pumped out of the body through tiny holes in the skin. Although you are only aware of sweating when you are very hot or the air is very moist, you are actually sweating all the time. Sweat consists mainly of water with salt and other waste chemicals dissolved in it.

Nearly two-thirds of your body is water. Some parts of the body contain more water than other parts. This chart shows the percentage of water in different parts of the body.

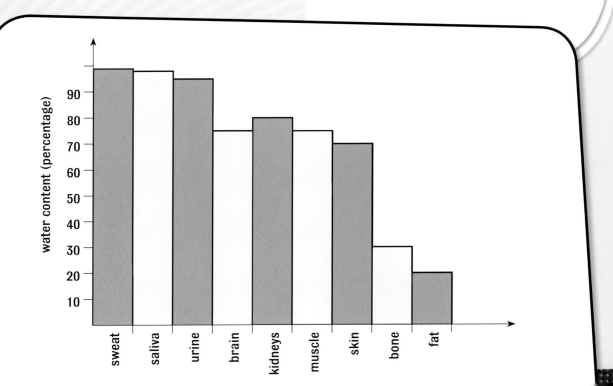

Water balance

Your body loses water all the time. It loses water just from breathing, but it loses most water in the form of urine and sweat. Altogether, you probably lose about 1–2 litres (1.8–3.5 pints) of water a day depending on the weather and how active you are. To replace the water lost, you take in new supplies of water every day in your food and by drinking. Your body has to balance the water lost with the water taken in.

Urine

Nearly half of all the water you lose is urine. How much urine your kidneys make depends on how much water you have drunk and how hot the weather is. The more you drink the more urine you make. However, when you are hot you lose more water as sweat. To keep the amount of water in your body balanced, your kidneys then produce less urine.

Sweating

Your body loses water through the skin all the time, but when you are hot you sweat much more. Sweating helps to cool your body down. The water is pumped on to your skin, but the heat of your body makes it evaporate. As it evaporates it takes heat from your blood.

Breathing out

When blood reaches your lungs, carbon dioxide and water **vapour** pass from the blood into the lungs. These two gases then leave the body with the air that you breathe out. Every day you breathe out the equivalent of 500 millilitres of water in the form of vapour.

If you breathe out on to a mirror, the mirror will mist up with water droplets. These droplets have **condensed** from water vapour in the air that you have just breathed out.

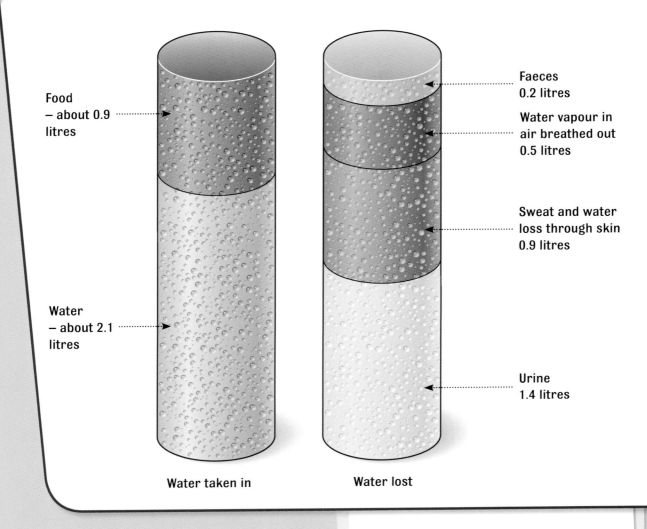

Food – about 0.9 litres

Water – about 2.1 litres

Faeces 0.2 litres

Water vapour in air breathed out 0.5 litres

Sweat and water loss through skin 0.9 litres

Urine 1.4 litres

Water taken in

Water lost

Faeces

Faeces contains water as well as fibre and waste materials. The water in faeces makes it soft and easier to push out of the body. Usually only about 6 per cent of the body's water is lost through faeces. If you have **diarrhoea**, however, a lot of extra water and salts may be lost. It is important to drink extra water to make up for any lost while suffering from diarrhoea.

 These tanks show how the amounts of water you take in and lose are made up. The more water you drink, the more you will lose as urine. This means the amount of water in your body stays about the same.

Thirst

Thirst is a strong signal that your body needs more water to balance the water lost. You feel thirsty when your mouth becomes drier because it is making less saliva. By this time, your body is really short of water. You should drink regularly throughout the day, so that your body does not have to send you this emergency signal!

Water in the kidneys

You have two kidneys, one on each side of the body just above your waist. They filter the blood and remove poisonous waste, such as **urea**, and excess water and salt. The water with salt and urea dissolved in it trickles from the kidneys down to the bladder, where it is stored.

Poisonous waste

The main ingredient of urea is **nitrogen**. The liver changes the body's waste nitrogen into urea, a solid that dissolves easily in the water in the blood. The liver also breaks down other poisons in the body and turns them into harmless waste chemicals. These include chemicals that you would not usually think of as poisons, for example, caffeine in cola.

In the kidneys

Each kidney is made up of over a million tiny filters called nephrons. As blood enters a filter, water and everything dissolved in it is forced out of the blood. Most of the water and all the dissolved food and nutrients pass through the filter and back into the blood. What remains is excess water with urea, salt, and waste chemicals dissolved in it. It is called urine and it moves down one of the tubes, called ureters, into the bladder.

About a quarter of your blood passes through your kidneys every minute. The kidneys clean the blood by filtering out poisonous chemicals and excess salt and water. This produces urine, which is stored in the bladder.

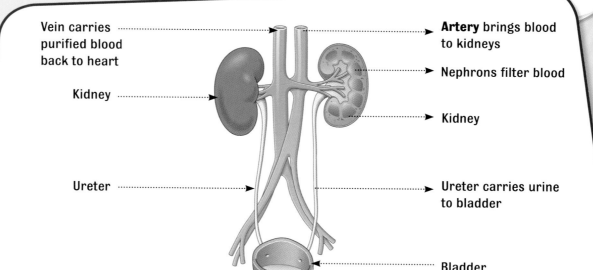

Vein carries purified blood back to heart

Kidney

Ureter

Artery brings blood to kidneys

Nephrons filter blood

Kidney

Ureter carries urine to bladder

Bladder

Urethra

Excess water

You may think that drinking extra water will make your kidneys work harder, but in fact extra water makes it easier for your kidneys. The more water there is in your blood, the more diluted the excess salt and other wastes become. This means that each filter has to deal with less salt and waste.

Urine

The kidneys send a constant trickle of urine into the bladder, where it is stored. As the bladder fills up with urine, it stretches. Nerves in the walls of the bladder alert your brain when you need to urinate. If you wait until your bladder is very full, the need to urinate will become desperate. The more liquid you drink, the more often you need to urinate.

Urinating

A ring of muscle at the bottom of the bladder usually keeps the bladder tightly closed. When you urinate, this muscle relaxes and urine flows out of your body from the bladder through a tube called the urethra.

Bladder fact

Your bladder can hold only about 0.5 litres (0.9 pints) of urine at a time, but your body makes about three times this amount every day. This means that you have to urinate several times a day.

 Babies cannot recognize when they need to urinate and cannot control the muscle that allows urine to leave the bladder. They wear nappies to absorb the urine instead.

Too little water

If you do not drink enough water, you become dehydrated. This makes it difficult for your body to get rid of the poisonous waste chemicals in your blood. If you do not drink enough for many hours you will become thirstier and thirstier as your body becomes increasingly desperate for water. People can survive for only a few days without water.

Dehydration

You do not always feel symptoms of mild dehydration, but as you become more dehydrated you begin to feel thirsty. If you do not drink you can begin to feel tired and dizzy. Dehydration can cause headaches and a dry mouth.

Sweating

Sweating also causes dehydration, so you should always drink more liquid in hot weather or when you are in a hot place. People who are exercising vigorously can lose up to 1.7 litres (3 pints) of sweat an hour and are particularly in danger of dehydration.

Severe dehydration

When someone suffers from severe dehydration, all of the tissues in their body become short of water and cannot function properly. Their heart starts to beat very fast and their **blood pressure** falls. If they do not get treatment they will go into **shock** and die.

 Tennis players often have to play hard in very hot weather. Players sip water in the breaks between games so they will not become dehydrated.

Dying of thirst

When you think of someone dying of thirst, you probably think of people stranded at sea or lost in the desert, but millions of people worldwide die of dehydration every year. Most of these deaths are due to dysentery, an infectious disease that causes severe diarrhoea. Other people die of dehydration when they lose a lot of blood or suffer burns that cover a large area of their body.

ANNALISE'S STORY

Annalise drank very little during the day, because she didn't like using the school toilets. Her skin was dry, she often had headaches, and felt tired and listless. Then she read on the Internet that these problems could be caused by dehydration. She carried a bottle of water to drink during the day. When she got home she drank lots of water. Her headaches have gone, she now feels more energetic, and her skin is no longer dry.

This person is very ill and has been taken to hospital. She has been put on a drip – a mixture of water, glucose, and salts. It is fed into her blood to stop her becoming dehydrated.

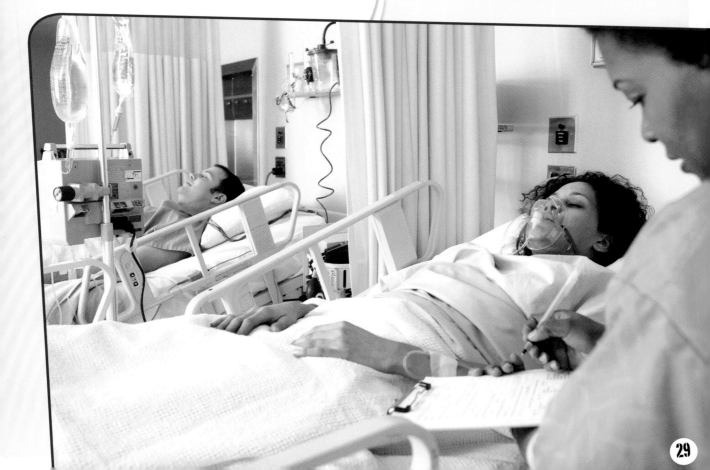

Too much water

In normal circumstances it is quite difficult to drink too much water. When you have drunk about a litre, your stomach will be full and you will not want to drink any more. The people who are most likely to drink too much water are those who are trying to avoid dehydration. When a person becomes overheated, they may overcorrect and drink far too much liquid. Too much water upsets the balance of water and salt in the body and, in extreme cases, can cause death.

Balancing water and salt

Salt controls how much water passes out of the blood into your tissues to keep them moist. Your kidneys normally make sure that your blood contains the right amount of salt and water. But if the blood contains too much water and not enough salt, water leaves the blood and floods the tissues of the body.

Overheating

Athletes and, more dangerously, people who take the illegal drug ecstasy are most at risk of overheating. When you become hot, your body sweats to cool you down. Sweat includes salt and water, so when you sweat your body loses both. Sweating usually keeps your temperature more or less constant, but sometimes people become so hot that sweating cannot cool them. Highly trained athletes should know how much water they need to drink to prevent overheating, but the drug ecstasy makes people think that everything is all right with the world, even when things are going dangerously wrong.

 Drinking water usually helps your kidneys to work better, but, if your kidneys cannot cope with it, excess water may flood your body.

Flooded with water

Several ecstasy users have died from drinking too much water when they were overheated. Ecstasy users are in danger of becoming dehydrated. However, if they drink litre after litre of water, the amount of salt in the body becomes too diluted. The drug ecstasy also stops the kidneys working. Instead of the extra water being extracted from the blood, it floods the body's tissues. Most damaging, the brain becomes swollen. As it swells, it is squashed by the bony skull that usually protects it. Pressure on the brain quickly leads to **coma** and death.

Safe amount to drink

Athletes, and anyone who is exercising vigorously or liable to become very hot, should drink about half a litre an hour. Sipping water or soft drinks will replace the water lost. Isotonic drinks, which are special drinks for athletes, are the best things to sip, because they include salts.

The effects of ecstasy and too much water in the body can have tragic consequences.

Too little fibre

If you do not eat enough fibre, your large intestine will work slowly and sluggishly. This may lead to constipation, which is difficulty in passing faeces. Over a long period of time, continual constipation leads to piles and possibly cancer of the large intestine.

Moving along

Fibre and food pass into the bowel (another name for the large intestine). Undigested food only moves through the bowel when the muscles of the tube tighten behind it and push it forward. The less undigested food there is in the large intestine, the less often the muscles contract. This means that undigested food stays in the bowel for much longer than it should.

 These foods contain almost no fibre. Only the tomato contains a little fibre. If you like to eat food like this, you should also include foods that are high in fibre, such as baked beans, wholemeal bread, and vegetables.

Constipation

How easy it is to push faeces out of the body depends on how much fibre and water the faeces contain. The longer the mushy paste stays in the bowel, the more water from it is absorbed back into the body. This means that the waste material becomes dry and hard, which makes it difficult and painful to push it out of the body.

RELIEVING CONSTIPATION

If you often suffer from constipation, you should eat more fibre and drink more water. A glass of lukewarm water first thing in the morning often helps. You can buy remedies for constipation from the chemist, but you should not use them all the time.

Testing transit time

Transit time is the time taken for undigested food to pass right through your body. It should be between 12 and 24 hours.
You can test your transit time by eating a lot of beetroot – it will dye your faeces red! See how long it takes for the undigested beetroot to pass out of your body. If it is more than 24 hours, you need to eat more fibre and drink more water.

Piles

Constipation is unpleasant and can build up trouble for the future. Adults who often suffer from constipation may develop piles. The blood vessels in the anus and rectum become stretched and swollen, like varicose veins. Piles are itchy and are painful, particularly when passing faeces.

Cancer of the bowel

Continual constipation over many years can lead to cancer of the bowel. People who live in Europe, Australia, and North America are more likely to get cancer of the bowel than people who live in Africa and Asia. This may be because most Africans and Asians have far more fibre in their diets.

Eating meals that contain plenty of fibre keeps the large intestine healthy and working well.

Too much fibre

Fibre in your diet makes your digestive system work more efficiently. Eating more fibre than you are used to can cause excess gas to build up, giving you wind and even diarrhoea. Too much fibre can also stop you getting enough nutrients if it fills your stomach and stops you eating more nutritious food. Some fibre actually prevents particular minerals being absorbed into the blood.

Gas in the large intestine

Adults normally have about 200 millilitres of gases in the digestive system, but children have a bit less. These gases come from various sources. Some of them are produced in the large intestine. There, billions of bacteria produce **methane**, carbon dioxide, and hydrogen as they feed on the undigested food. These gases have a foul smell and may be passed as wind or when you go to the toilet.

Indigestion

Fibre is difficult to digest, so if you eat a lot of it, your system may be unable to digest it all, giving you indigestion. More undigested food in the large intestine gives the bacteria there more to feed on and so they produce more gas. Some foods, such as beans, cabbage, cauliflower, onions, and garlic, make more gas than others. The extra gases fill the digestive tube, making your **abdomen** sore and swollen. Chewing your food for longer helps to prevent indigestion and reduces excess wind.

This girl has just eaten a meal that contained too much fibre. Now her abdomen is sore because her intestines are swollen with gas.

Irritable gut

Too much fibre can make your digestive tubes inflamed and irritable. Apart from causing pain, food is pushed through the intestines too quickly, so there is not enough time for the water to be absorbed through the wall of the large intestine into the blood. Extra water in the faeces makes it very loose and runny, producing diarrhoea.

Replacing nutrients

Young children in particular should not eat too much fibre because it might replace nutritious food. It fills their stomach so that they stop eating before they have taken in enough carbohydrates, fats, proteins, and other nutrients.

Minerals

The fibre contained in the outer skins of wholemeal cereals prevents some minerals, particularly calcium, iron, and zinc, from being absorbed into the blood. Children in particular should not eat a lot of raw bran.

>> **GAS IN THE STOMACH**

Most of the gas in your stomach is air that you swallow with your food. It can also include carbon dioxide from fizzy drinks. If there is too much gas in your stomach, you usually burp to get rid of some of it.

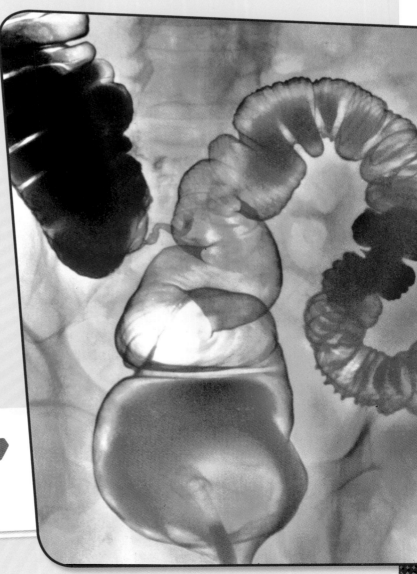

Intestines can become inflamed and cause discomfort if the wrong amount of fibre is eaten. >>

Healthy eating

Just as it is important to eat enough, but not too much, fibre, it is also important to eat enough, but not too much, of each kind of nutrient — carbohydrates, proteins, fats, vitamins, and minerals. Eating the right amount of all these kinds of foods means you have a balanced diet.

The eatwell plate

Different kinds of foods are rich in different nutrients. The eatwell plate divides food into five main groups. It shows the kinds of food you should eat most of, and the kinds you should only eat a little of.

1 – Bread, rice, potatoes, and pasta

These foods are rich in carbohydrates and so give you energy. About one-third of all the food you eat should come from this group. If you choose wholemeal bread, pasta, and flour, you will get lots of fibre, too. Muesli and porridge oats are two breakfast cereals that contain a good quantity of fibre, but do not eat too many of those that contain bran.

2 – Fruit and vegetables

Fruit and vegetables are rich in vitamins, minerals, and fibre. Fruit and vegetables should make up another third of your diet. Try to eat at least five portions of fruit and vegetables every day. All types of fruit and vegetables count towards this amount.

3 – Meat, fish, eggs, and beans

This group includes eggs and pulses, as well as meat and fish. These foods are all rich in protein, but, apart from pulses, they contain no fibre. Nevertheless, protein is very important, particularly for children who are still growing. You can easily make up the fibre from other kinds of food.

4 – Milk and dairy foods

Milk and dairy foods, including cheese and yoghurt, are rich in protein, vitamins, and minerals (particularly calcium), although many contain quite a lot of fat and no fibre. It is important to eat some dairy food every day, but, if you are overweight, you should choose special varieties that are lower in fat, such as semi-skimmed milk and low-fat yoghurts.

5 – Food full of fat or sugar

Fatty and sugary foods include chocolate, sweets, cakes, sausages, crisps, fizzy drinks, and many other popular snacks. They contain little or no fibre. Too much sugar and fat is bad for your health, so you should eat only a very small amount of these foods.

RULES FOR HEALTHY EATING

- Eat a wide variety of food.
- Eat most food from groups 1 and 2.
- Eat only a little food from group 5.

The eatwell plate divides food into five main groups. This plate shows which groups you should eat most food from and which groups you should eat the least food from.

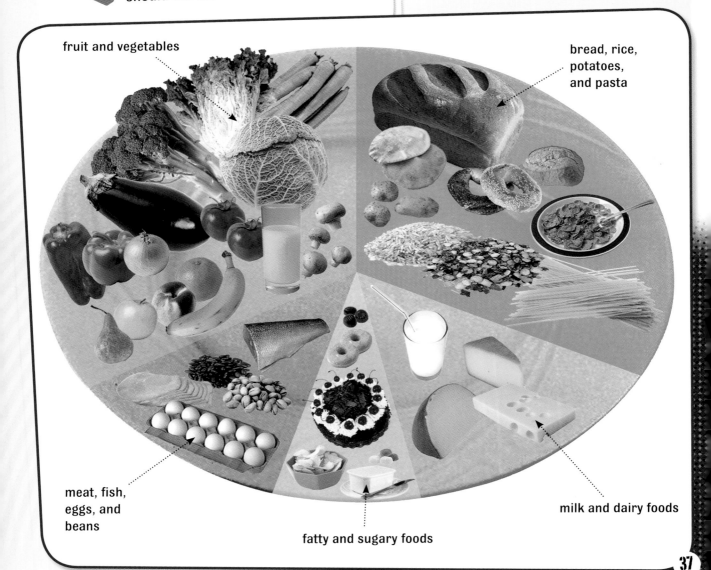

fruit and vegetables

bread, rice, potatoes, and pasta

meat, fish, eggs, and beans

fatty and sugary foods

milk and dairy foods

Healthy drinking

Most people lose about 1.2 litres (2 pints) of water a day, mostly in the form of urine and sweat. You need to take in enough water to replace the amount lost. Your body gets nearly a third of the water it needs from food but the rest must come from drinks. This means that most people should drink about 6–8 glasses of fluid a day.

Water in food and drinks

If you follow the eatwell plate, you will absorb water from the fruit and vegetables you eat every day, as well as from bread, pasta, rice, and potatoes. All food has some water in it, otherwise it would be too dry to eat.

This girl is enjoying a slice of watermelon. It contains a lot of juice and will help to replace some of the water she loses during the day.

Soup and all drinks are mainly water. Some, such as tea, are made by adding water, but others, such as milk, are already made mainly of water. You can replace the liquid your body loses by drinking fruit juices and milk, but it is particularly helpful to your body if you also drink plain water.

Caffeine

Cola, tea, and coffee all contain a substance called caffeine. Caffeine speeds up the processes in the body and makes you feel more alert. It also makes your kidneys produce more urine, so they extract more water from your blood. Most people can tolerate a certain amount of caffeine without becoming dehydrated. However, when you consume more caffeine than you are used to this can cause mild dehydration.

Alcohol

Alcohol in large amounts can be dehydrating. People who have drunk a lot of alcohol often suffer from a hangover afterwards. Their mouth feels dry, their head may ache, and they may feel tired and sick. Most of these symptoms are caused by dehydration — just one of many problems caused by drinking alcohol.

Women can drink up to 2 to 3 units of alcohol a day and men up to 3 to 4 units a day, without a major risk to their health. A unit is half a pint of standard strength beer, lager, or cider, or a pub measure of spirit. A glass of wine is about 2 units and alcopops are about 1.5 units. Pregnant women should not drink alcohol at all.

The bottle of water shows you how much liquid you should drink every day. The glasses show one way of drinking this amount of liquid. Remember that you cannot count cola, tea, or coffee.

Healthy diets

Your diet consists of all the foods you usually eat. Many people in Western countries, including Europe, Australia, and North America, eat a diet that is too low in fibre. People from other parts of the world eat food that usually contains much more fibre. Vegetarians and vegans follow special diets, but these diets usually contain plenty of fibre.

Traditional diets

Most people in western countries use flour refined from wheat, but people in Africa, Asia, and South America often make flour from other grains, such as maize and rice, and this flour is less refined. Their diets often include beans, peas, or lentils, which are cheap and rich in nutrients and fibre. Traditional recipes from these areas are becoming more popular, as people realize how healthy and tasty they are.

Vegetarian and vegan diets

Vegetarians do not eat meat and often do not eat fish either. Vegans exclude any food that has come from animals, including milk and all other dairy food. Vegetarian diets may be more healthy than meat diets because they are more likely to be high in fibre and low in fat. Vegan diets are also usually rich in fibre, but vegans have to choose their food carefully to make sure they get all the nutrients they need.

These children are enjoying couscous, a traditional meal from North Africa. It includes chickpeas and meat in a spicy sauce and is served with semolina, a grain that is rich in fibre.

BEN'S STORY

Ben liked to eat chips, sausages, burgers, and chocolate, but his doctor told him that he was getting too fat. Ben changed his diet. He stopped eating such fatty food and ate wholemeal bread and spaghetti instead. The fibre in the food stopped him feeling hungry. He also drank plenty of water to help make him feel full. When he wanted a snack he had a banana, apple, or raw carrot. He joined a sports club at school. He became fitter and healthy, and soon lost all the excess weight.

People who are ill

People who are ill often do not feel like eating very much. It is, however, particularly important that they do not stop drinking. If you are vomiting or suffering from diarrhoea, you need to drink plenty of water or other fluids to replace the extra water lost. Similarly, if you have a high temperature, or a fever, you need to drink plenty of extra water to replace all the water lost through sweating.

When you have a high temperature or a sore throat, you may not feel like eating very much, but it is very important that you drink plenty of water.

Daily requirements

In Western countries most people eat about 12 grams (0.4 ounces) of fibre a day, but scientists recommend that adults should have 18 grams (0.6 ounces) a day. Children should have less, depending on their weight. For example, if you weigh about 33 kilograms (73 pounds) then you should have about 9 grams (0.3 ounces) of fibre, half the amount for an adult. Young children should have much less fibre. In the same way, while adults should drink 6 to 8 glasses of liquid a day, you can reduce this amount if you weigh less.

Food		Amount that gives 10 grams of fibre
Fruit	Apples	3–4 apples
	Bananas	3 bananas
	Oranges	3 oranges
Vegetables	Broccoli	1 large head
	Cabbage	1 medium cabbage
	Carrots	5 carrots
Pulses	Baked beans	1 small can
	Lentils (cooked)	125 grams
	Peas (boiled)	200 grams
Cereals	Cornflakes	10 cups
	Oat cakes	10 biscuits
	White bread	15 slices
	Wholemeal bread	5 slices
Potatoes	Baked jacket potato	1 large
	Boiled new potatoes	7 potatoes

Amount of fibre and water in different foods

Food	Amount of fibre in 100 grams	Amount of water in 100 grams
Apples, including skin	1.8 g	85 ml
Baked beans	3.7 g	72 ml
Bananas	3.4 g	75 ml
Boiled egg	0 g	75 ml
Cheddar cheese	0 g	36 ml
Chocolate (most)	0 g	0.9 ml
Cooked white spaghetti	1.2 g	73.8 ml
Corn flakes	2.5 g	3 ml
Cucumber	0.6 g	96 ml
Fish	0 g	65–75 ml
Meat	0 g	40–70 ml
Oven chips	2 g	59 ml
Peanut butter	5.4 g	1 ml
Peas	4.7 g	78 ml
Plain sponge cake	0.9 g	20 ml
Raw tomatoes	1 g	93 ml
Semi-skimmed milk	0 g	90 ml
Weetabix®	9.7 g	6 ml
White bread	2.5 g	37 ml
Wholemeal bread	7 g	38 ml

This meal contains 7.3 grams (0.26 ounces) of fibre and 289 grams (10 ounces) of water (that is 289 millilitres of water).

Glossary

abdomen   belly, the part of the body that contains the stomach and small intestines

amino acids   building blocks of protein. Different amino acids combine together to form a protein.

arteries   tubes that carry blood from the heart to different parts of the body

bacteria   single, living cells. Most kinds of bacteria are harmless, but some kinds can cause disease.

blood pressure   pressure the blood puts on the walls of blood vessels as it is pumped round the body. Blood pressure changes depending on the force of the heartbeat.

calcium   simple substance, found in the earth and in foods such as milk and cheese. Your body needs calcium for strong, healthy bones and teeth.

carbohydrates   substances in food that your body uses to provide energy. Foods that contain a lot of carbohydrates include bread, rice, potatoes, and sugar.

carbon dioxide   one of the gases in air. Plants take in carbon dioxide to make food and they produce oxygen as a result, one of the things that humans need to survive.

cell   smallest living unit. The body is made up of many different kinds of cells, such as bone cells, blood cells, and skin cells.

cellulose   substance that the walls of plants cells are made of

cholesterol   substance made by the body and found in some foods. It is necessary for certain functions of the body, but can lead to health problems if too much cholesterol is formed and deposited on the walls of blood vessels.

chyme   mushy liquid that passes from the stomach to the small intestine. It is formed from partly digested food mixed with the digestive juices of the stomach.

coma   state of deep sleep from which the patient cannot wake up. Comas can continue for a long time.

condensed   when a gas or a vapour, such as water vapour, cools and changes into a liquid

dehydrated   when the body has less water than it needs

diarrhoea   faeces that are loose and watery

digest   process of breaking down food when it is eaten. Digestion starts in the mouth when you bite and chew food and continues until the molecules that make up food are taken into the bloodstream.

dissolve   when a solid or gas merges with a liquid

element   simple substance that cannot be broken up into any other substances

energy   ability to do work or to make something happen

enzyme   substance that helps a chemical change take place faster without being changed itself

evaporate   when a solid or a liquid becomes a gas

faeces   undigested food, bacteria, digestive juices, and dead cells that are excreted as solid waste

fat   substance that the body can change into energy. A layer of fat under the skin helps to keep the body warm.

fungi   group of living things that includes mushrooms, yeasts, and moulds

glucose   type of sugar

glycogen   name for any glucose stored in the liver and muscles following absorption. Extra glucose is stored if it is not needed immediately by the body.

gravity   way that everything is attracted downwards, towards the ground

hydrogen   invisible gas that is one of the gases in the air. Hydrogen combines with other substances to form, for example, water, sugar, proteins, and fats.

insoluble fibre   fibre that is unable to dissolve in a liquid

iron   simple substance found in the earth. Your body needs iron so that red blood cells can carry oxygen.

large intestine   part of the intestines through which undigested food passes after it has left the small intestine

liver   body organ that produces digestive juices

methane   gas that occurs naturally in the earth and is made in the body in the large intestine

mineral   non-living substance found in the ground. Your body needs certain minerals to function healthily.

molecule   smallest part of a substance that can exist and still be that substance

mucus   slimy liquid made in the body

neutralize   to make something neutral, that is, neither acid nor alkaline

nitrogen   invisible gas that is the main gas in the air. Nitrogen combines with other substances in all the different tissues in your body.

nutrients   parts of food that your body needs to get energy, to build and repair cells, and for the cells to function properly. Nutrients include carbohydrates, fats, proteins, vitamins, and minerals.

oesophagus   tube through which food travels from the mouth to the stomach

organ   part of the body that does a particular job. The heart, stomach, and intestines are all organs.

oxygen invisible gas that is one of the gases in air. The body needs oxygen in order to break down sugar to form energy.

pancreas gland that produces various digestive juices that flow through a tube into the small intestine

pharynx part of the throat where the tubes to the nose, lungs, and stomach begin

phosphorus simple substance that is needed for plants to grow

pollutant something that poisons air, water, or soil. A pollutant is often a waste material.

proteins complex chemicals that the body needs to grow and repair cells

pulses group of foods that includes lentils, peas, and beans. Pulses are the seeds of some plants and are rich in protein.

recycled reused, sometimes in another form

saliva watery liquid made by glands in your mouth and the inside of your cheeks

sediments solid particles that collect at the bottom of a container of liquid

shock condition caused by a fall in blood pressure that can lead to a person becoming unconscious

small intestine part of the intestine into which food passes from the stomach to be digested and absorbed into the blood. Undigested food passes right through the small intestine into the large intestine.

soluble fibre fibre that dissolves in water and passes into the blood

urea substance formed from waste material in the liver

urine liquid filtered out of the blood by the kidneys as waste and excreted as a yellowish liquid. Urine consists of urea mixed with excess salt and water.

vapour gas that rises from a liquid or solid

vitamins chemicals that your body needs to stay healthy

zinc mineral that the body needs to grow and to help wounds heal

Find out more

Books

Break It Down: The Digestive System, Steve Parker (Raintree, 2006)

Graphing Food and Nutrition, Isabel Thomas (Heinemann Library, 2008)

What's On Your Plate? Dinner, Lola M. Schaefer and A. Ted Schaefer (Raintree, 2006)

Websites

www.bbc.co.uk/health/nutrition
Investigate nutrition and healthy living on this website.

www.mckinley.uiuc.edu/Handouts/sports_nutrition.html
This site tells you about drinking fluid, and is especially useful if you are an athlete or highly active.

www.mckinley.uiuc.edu/Handouts/high_fiber.htm
This site tells you about fibre and gives examples of the amounts of fibre in different kinds of food.

www.NutritionAustralia.org
This is the information service of the Australian Nutrition Foundation.

www.nutrition.org.uk/
Website of the British Nutrition Foundation, which gives information on all aspects of diet, including fibre. Click on "Healthy eating" to get started.

www.talktofrank.com/drugs.aspx?id=180
On this website you can find out more about water in relation to the drug ecstasy.

Index